Antonio's Rainforest

BY ANNA LEWINGTON
PHOTOGRAPHS BY EDWARD PARKER

Wayland

Editor: Catherine Ellis
Designer: Joyce Chester
Reprinted in 1998 by
Wayland Publishers Limited
61 Western Road, Hove
East Sussex, BN3 1JD, England

Find Wayland on the Internet at http://www.wayland.co.uk

British Library Cataloguing in Publication Data

Lewington, Anna
Antonio's Rainforest
I. Title
574.5
ISBN 0 7502 2321 9

Typeset by Dorchester Typesetting Group Ltd
Printed in Italy by G. Canale & C. S. p. A., Turin

Contents

Preface

Antonio's Rainforest tells the story of a rubber tapper family living in the forests of western Amazonia, in Brazil. Brazil is an enormous and wonderful country. Half of it is covered by forest, the largest forest in the world – in fact, you could fit the whole of Europe into Brazilian Amazonia alone!

This book is based on real events that took place in the Alto Jurua Valley, in the state of Acre. It was there that many brave people, led by a man called Macedo, got together to fight against exploitation by the rubber barons (the *patrões*), and to protect the forest. They put together a community plan for the future of the region. Their activities were a success, and in January 1990 the president of Brazil officially declared the Alto Jurua region to be an extractive reserve. That means the forest cannot be cut down by loggers, who want to make money out of the wood, or by ranchers, who want to raise cattle on the land.

Later in 1990, in response to an invitation from Macedo, Anna Lewington and Edward Parker visited the reserve on behalf of WWF–UK. There they met the Antonio of this book, and talked to the rubber tappers about their community plan. The rubber tappers need money to help them set up their own co-operative, for trading rubber and storing goods, and to set up schools and health posts for the families living in the reserve.

In 1991 WWF contributed funding for part of the rubber tappers' plan, and it has promised further help. WWF is convinced that, in order to protect tropical forests, we must support the local people and their way of life. Rubber tappers have shown that they are truly guardians of the forest. By living in small communities and collecting rubber and other products from the trees, they have prevented large areas of forest from being destroyed, and many species of plants and animals from being over-exploited. It is very important that the rubber tappers' way of life continues. More and more rubber plantations are being created in Brazil, outside Amazonia, and these may threaten the existence of rubber tapper communities, and therefore the future of the forest.

The names of the people and places in this book have been changed, because there are still some people who don't want the rubber tappers to protect the forest as they do. However, Antonio is a real little boy, and by helping him secure his future we are helping to make sure the rainforest survives.

Sandra Charity, Latin America Conservation Officer, WWF–UK

SOUTH AMERICA

CENTRAL
AMERICA

TRINIDAD AND TOBAGO

PANAMA

VENEZUELA

GUYANA

COLOMBIA

FRENCH
GUIANA

SURINAM

Branco

Negro

Equator

ECUADOR

Manaus

Amazon

Belém

Juruá

Madeira

Tapajós

Cruzeiro do Sul

Purus

ALTO JURUA EXTRACTIVE RESERVE

Xingu

PERU

B R A Z I L

BOLIVIA

Brasília

PARAGUAY

PACIFIC OCEAN

São Paulo

Rio de Janeiro

C
H
I
L
E

URUGUAY

ATLANTIC OCEAN

ARGENTINA

0		200		400	miles
0	200	400	600	800 km	

Antonio's home

My name is Antonio José and I live in the rainforest, in Brazil. My father is a rubber tapper, a *seringueiro*. He collects the white sap from the wild rubber trees that grow in the forest around here, near the Armadillo river, and I help him.

I have got one little brother: Chico, who's just six months old; and two sisters: Maria Aparecida who's five and Maria Nazaré who's three. Because I'm the oldest – I'm eight now – I help my mother with little Chico, and I hold him when she's sweeping the floor or fetching water. Because our house is raised up off the ground we have to make sure Chico doesn't fall out. He did once and burst into tears because our black pigs trotted out from under the house and started snuffling round him.

We have lived here for as long as I can remember, but my dad was born in Paraíso,

This is me, Antonio José, in our house.

Above Here is my family outside our house. Dad is holding Maria Nazaré, mum is holding Chico, and Maria Aparecida is standing next to me.

Right Our two black pigs crunch up pieces of manioc for breakfast.

on the other side of the Armadillo river, and my mum used to live at Foz do Jacaré. That's a really long way from here. If my dad sets off in the morning to carry the rubber he has collected to the community warehouse at Foz do Jacaré, the sun is just above the banana trees outside our house. When he gets back, the sun is going down behind the *buriti* palm and the tinamou (a kind of bird) is calling out.

I've only been to Foz do Jacaré twice. The first time was four years ago, when I was very small, and dad started going to lots of meetings there. The rubber tappers from all around the Armadillo river were trying to work out how they could be free of their bosses, called the *patrões*, who made them collect rubber for nothing and who were

The discovery of rubber

The rubber that is used today to make tyres for bicycles and cars, lorries and aeroplanes was first used by the Amerindians of South and Central America. They made balls and shoes and bags from rubber, and even syringes – which is where *seringa*, the Portuguese word for rubber, comes from.

The Amerindians discovered how to extract the sap, or latex, from rubber trees by cutting the bark and fixing little gourd cups to each one. They thickened the sap by passing it through smoke and made it into different shapes by moulding it.

European explorers copied the Amerindians and brought this new substance back from Brazil. In the eighteenth century they began experimenting with it to see what they could make. One of the first things they found was that lumps of the dry sap would rub out pencil marks, and this is how 'rubber' got its name.

Collecting latex from a Brazilian forest, in the late nineteenth century.

threatening to cut all the forest down. The second time I went to Foz do Jacaré was two years ago when this forest was officially declared an extractive reserve by the Brazilian Government. Everybody celebrated because, after all the work my dad and the others had done, this whole forest area was finally ours, for all the rubber tappers to use and to protect for ever.

I liked Foz do Jacaré, but I like it better here. Over there, the old *patrões* cut down so many trees there is hardly any shelter from the sun or rain. When it rains the ground turns into a sea of slippery mud, but when it stops the sun is so fierce that it makes the

dusty orange soil too hot to stand on. That can be a problem because we don't have any proper shoes, though my dad does have a pair of rubber boots.

I like the forest because it's cooler, but we have to be careful not to tread on *tucandera* ants. They are the biggest ants in the forest and when they sting you the pain is dreadful. If we do get stung mum makes up some tea from avocado stones, and after a while the swelling goes down.

Luckily, we've got an avocado tree just by the house. When the fruit are ripe my cousin Raimundo, who lives just down the path, comes over and helps me knock them down. It's good fun. We call him *catipuru*, which means tree squirrel, because he is always the first one up the tree.

This map shows the rivers in our reserve and where we live.

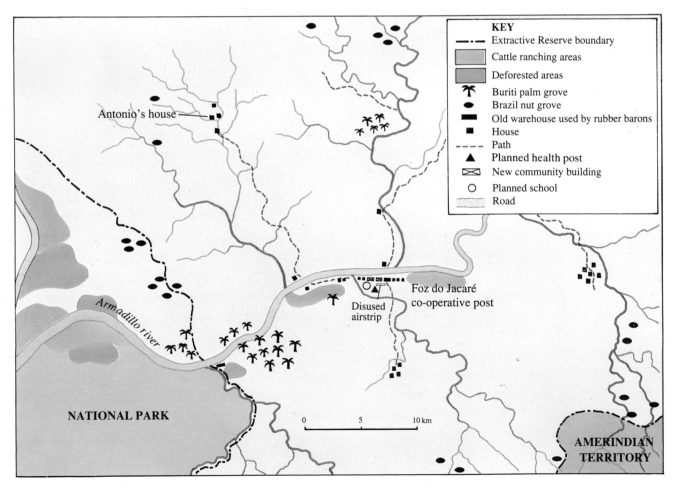

José with the wooden aeroplane his dad made. The propeller spins round when you run.

Raimundo is my best friend, but we don't get much time to play because we're usually helping with chores around the house. Both of us help look after our brothers and sisters, and I help dad collecting rubber too. We don't have many toys, but sometimes we borrow the wooden aeroplane that my friend José's dad made.

Sometimes you can hear real aeroplanes humming in the distance, like a swarm of bees. I saw one once from our manioc garden where there's a big gap in the trees. It flew low over the forest towards Foz do Jacaré, but the landing strip there is all overgrown, so I don't know where it landed. Da Silva, the rich rubber boss, built that landing strip. He was the one who used to force my dad to give him all the rubber he could collect. Now that this whole area of forest has been made a reserve, Da Silva has left. My dad's friends, who are all rubber tappers too, are going to try and remake the landing strip so that planes can bring in some of the things we need, and can take people to Cruzeiro do Sul – our nearest town – in emergencies.

It takes four days to get to Cruzeiro do Sul and back by boat when the Armadillo river is high and flowing fast, and seven days or more when the river is low, in the dry season. There are no roads through our forest. That's what dad and all the others worked so hard to stop.

10

Our struggle against Da Silva began when he tried to sell this forest to a company who wanted to cut all the trees down. Just imagine! They were going to bring great big machines in to push down the trees and carve a road right through, past Foz do Jacaré. All this forest would have gone, with about 500 families in it. All the rubber and brazil nut trees, the palms, fruit trees, the giant mahogany and *canela* trees with their cinnamon-scented bark would have been destroyed. And all the animals and birds!

Da Silva was going to turn all this forest into one big ranch, with cattle feeding off the straggly grass. And where would we have gone? Dad says we would have had to go to Cruzeiro do Sul and beg. So we are lucky that the rubber tappers here could make their voices heard, and that the government listened to them and made our forest into a reserve for all the *seringueiros* of the Armadillo river.

Left My friend Raimundo's house is just along the path from us.

Below The Armadillo river, which runs through our reserve.

Who are rubber tappers?

About 150 years ago many people began to move into the Amazon forest from other parts of Brazil, and even other countries, to see if they could make a living as rubber tappers (*seringueiros*).

Life was very hard for them because each one had to work for a *patrão*, or boss, who demanded many kilos of rubber in return for the knife, clothes and food he gave them when they started. He also exchanged goods like salt, sugar and gunpowder, which he brought up the river with him from the nearest town – usually many days away. The problem was that the *patrão* was often unfair and asked for more rubber than was reasonable in exchange. So many rubber tappers could never get out of debt.

Antonio's grandfather came from northern Brazil to the Armadillo river in the western Amazon in 1940. Lots of rubber was needed at that time to make tyres for the aeroplanes and lorries used in the Second World War, and Antonio's grandfather wanted a good job.

Nineteenth century Amerindians in the rubber forest with their overseer. Their bosses treated them like slaves.

We use the forest to get nearly everything we need. Our houses are built from three different sorts of palm: we use the wood from one for the floor, and the bark from another for the walls. Our thatched roof is made from the great big leaf fronds of the *jaçi* palm, which you have to tie down one over the other with monkey-tail vines. There are lots of different palm trees in the forest, and many of them have delicious fruits. Mum makes drinks from *buriti* and *patoá*. *Patoá* is my favourite.

We grow nearly all our food in two gardens in the forest. We grow manioc (a bit like potatoes), maize and rice, and we get beans from Aunt Neorina because she can grow them on the bank of the Armadillo river. We've got sugar-cane growing by the

This is Raimundo's mother holding his little sister Simoni in their manioc garden. We call this tall variety of manioc mulatinha.

side of the house which we like to chew on, but we get our sugar for cooking from the new co-operative shop at Foz do Jacaré. Dad can also get cooking pots and clothes from the shop. But we don't get new things very often, because dad has to collect such a lot of rubber before he can exchange it for anything.

But now I'll take you into the forest, along the trail to my friend José's house. Maybe we'll see the armadillo, that lives in a burrow near the stream, and the capuchin monkeys in the cashew nut trees.

The trail begins just here.

13

Along the forest trail

My dad made our longest trail before I was born. It took him a long time because he was working on his own and he had only his machete to cut the undergrowth and saplings with. He didn't cut any big trees down, like the mahogany and cedars that grow all around here – you need lots of people to do that. He just cut a path between one rubber tree and the next.

We've got three trails all together, but to walk round the longest trail takes a whole day. It goes in a big loop from our house through the forest, ending up back here again. On my own I only go as far as José's house, which is just down by the stream.

When anyone is going to another person's house or coming back from the forest, we call through the trees: 'I'm co-m-ing!' stretching the word out so that we can be heard from a long way off. It is our way of letting one another know that we are all right and announcing where we are. We always keep our ears open because birds in the forest announce things too. When *pica pau*, the woodpecker, calls out in front of the house, dad says it's letting us know that people are coming to visit.

Bird-calls tell us lots of things. When the *uru* bird starts to sing we know that the summer (which is the dry season for us) has

Below This is my father. His name is Antonio too. He has been a rubber tapper ever since he was ten years old. He knows the forest well and has made three long trails so that he can tap the rubber trees.

Left My Uncle Raimundão can imitate bird and animal calls exactly. Here he is imitating a capuchin monkey.

Below This is part of our longest rubber trail. It takes a day to walk right round.

arrived. The tinamou sings every day at exactly the same time. When mum hears it she knows that it will soon be dark and that it is time to get the evening meal. The tinamou has another song as well, that tells us when it's going to rain. I like listening to the woodpeckers calling out to each other high up in the trees, from different parts of the forest. When one stops another one starts, a long way away, and they go on and on like that, calling and then answering each other back. Uncle Raimundão can imitate them perfectly. When he does the *uru* bird, no one can tell whether it's him or the bird!

The forest is the home of so many different birds and animals. I like walking along the trail because you never know which one you'll meet next. Some are easier to find than others. Armadillos are very shy and difficult to see because they only come out at night, but there are plenty of noisy monkeys around here. The howler monkeys make a tremendous din and so do the woolly monkeys. The capuchin monkeys are quieter – there's the brown one and the white-fronted capuchin – but they're much smaller and they disappear among the tree-tops very fast.

When I arrive at José's house we sometimes go and look for turtles together in the stream. But we have to be careful. Sting rays hide just beneath the surface of the sand on the stream bed. Their colour matches the sand exactly. If you are unlucky and you tread on one, it will lash round and jab your foot with the poisonous spine on the end of

Left There are many different kinds of monkey in our forest. This is the brown capuchin. We often see them scurrying through the trees throwing down bits of fruit and leaves as they go.

Right We use medicinal plants to treat almost all our illnesses, aches and pains. This is *capim santo*. We use its lemon-flavoured leaves to make a tea which helps cure fevers.

Below The *tucandera* ant is the biggest ant in the forest. We try hard to avoid them because their sting is so painful. This one stung my dad while he was tapping rubber.

its tail. The pain is much worse than a *tucandera* ant sting, and it lasts for many days. It's so bad, in fact, that it stops you from walking and you have to lie down and rest with your foot up. José trod on one last summer and his foot swelled up like a gourd. He drank lots of avocado stone tea, but it didn't help that much, so Mazí, his dad, went off and got some fruit from the *embauba* trees down by the Armadillo river. They made up a special remedy using the fruit and it helped to make the pain go away.

17

Mazí learned that remedy from the Kampa. They are an Amerindian group who live to the south and east of our reserve. Mazí said that they've got cures for all sorts of things. The Kampa are very friendly to us now. Like us, they've been having trouble defending their forest from settlers and logging companies, and some of them came to the meetings we held at Foz do Jacaré a while ago.

We learned most of what we know about living in the forest from the Amerindians.

They've been living here for thousands of years. Dad said it was Amerindians who taught his father how to track animals and to understand the things they do. They showed him how to use lots of the plants and trees here in the forest too. We use nearly all the trees along the trails, and if we don't use them the animals do. We eat the fruit from lots of different kinds of palm tree. Many of them contain oil that you can press out and use for cooking, and a milk you can use for seasoning food.

This is the *buriti* palm behind our house. You can see the fruits hanging down around the trunk. When they're ripe they turn yellow inside and are delicious to eat.

18

Antonio's forest trails

The diagram below shows the three forest trails Antonio's father has made so that he can collect the rubber latex from the trees. It also shows Antonio's house and the position of the family's gardens.

You can see the trails made by the other families at Mato Grosso too, and how they stretch out in big loops into the forest. One trail often leads on to another. Most families make at least two trails, or *estradas* as they are called in Brazil. Some are longer than others, but they can connect up to 200 wild rubber trees each.

The trail shown in detail here passes 120 rubber trees and takes Antonio's father about seven hours to walk round. There are lots of other trees along the trail that the rubber tappers use, including palms and hardwoods and many useful vines.

Antonio's family has two small gardens in the forest. The main crops grown are manioc and maize, but they plant lots of different fruit trees too. After two or three years the gardens are abandoned and left to grow back into forest, but the fruit trees are still harvested for many years to come.

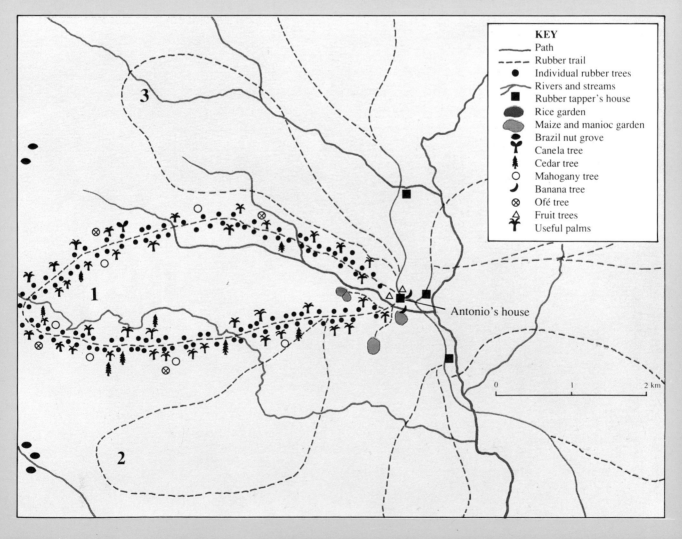

KEY
- Path
- Rubber trail
- ● Individual rubber trees
- Rivers and streams
- ■ Rubber tapper's house
- Rice garden
- Maize and manioc garden
- Brazil nut grove
- Canela tree
- Cedar tree
- ○ Mahogany tree
- Banana tree
- ⊗ Ofé tree
- △ Fruit trees
- Useful palms

Antonio's house

0   1   2 km

Left This is part of a huge cedar tree. It is being sawn into planks which will be used for some of the new buildings at Foz do Jacaré.

Right We use the vines that grow here in the forest in many different ways. This one is monkey-tail vine and we make a special tea from it.

The big trees that grow along the trail are also important to us. The timber of some of them – like cedar – is especially good for making canoes, and others, like *sapota,* are good for building with. We don't cut them down very often though, and when we do everybody lends a hand.

There are lots of useful vines in the forest. I can recognize six different kinds now. We use some of them, like *açu* and *titica,* for tying things and making sieves, baskets and brooms, and others for medicines. We make monkey-tail vine tea to help cure diarrhoea, and use the *ambé* vine for *tucandera* ant stings.

Even the stinging *tucandera* ants help us in their own way. When we see them scurrying along the path clutching their babies above their heads, it's a sure sign that it's going to rain hard. It won't rain on the same day you see them, but on the next one or the day after that. They're moving their babies from their nests to take them to higher, safer ground, because they know there's going to be a flood.

Although we have some rain the whole year round, most of it falls during the rainy season. When it rains then – between November and April – it really pours! As well as the *tucandera* ants, one other little animal warns us about the rain – the *jacuruxi* lizard. These lizards like to climb up the trunks of the trees down by the river and chirrup. All the *seringueiros* say that when you see a *jacuruxi* singing up a tree, its position marks how high the river will rise that year in the rainy season.

So you see, everything in the forest is useful for us. But dad still has to work extremely hard, tapping and collecting rubber, all day and every day.

I'll show you how it's done.

Tapping rubber

Along each of our three forest trails there are more than 100 rubber trees, (or *seringueira* trees, as we call them). My dad's work is to collect some of the milk-white sap from each one and bring it home to turn it into solid rubber blocks.

Because there are so many *seringueira* trees and the trails are so long, dad has to leave home very early in the morning. Sometimes he starts out before the sun is up, at four or five o'clock. He always takes his special knife, the *faca de seringa*, with him, and he also takes his gun.

This is dad walking along one of our trails on his way to tap the rubber trees.

There are several different stages to tapping rubber. The first stage is to prepare the surface of each tree by scraping away the rough top layer of the bark with a knife, making it smooth and flat. The next stage is to make a cut in the bark three or four days later. Dad makes a single diagonal cut around the tree and immediately the groove fills up with the thick white sap – the rubber latex. He quickly fixes a little tin cup to the bottom of the groove by sticking the sharpened lip into the bark. In this way he catches the trickle of latex as it flows out and down the groove.

Dad has to do this for each tree on each trail. He can do it very fast now, but it takes a while to learn how to cut the bark properly. There's a special way to hold the knife so that you make a nice straight groove. You have to be careful not to make the cut too deep, as this would damage the tree permanently and it might die.

Some of the rubber trees in this forest are very old. The *seringueiros* only ever tap the same part of a tree twice during its lifetime. They wait until the bark has fully regrown before they cut over the old grooves again, one line at a time, in the opposite direction.

Above Here you can see latex trickling out of the groove into a little tin cup.

Left Dad cuts a single sloping groove in the bark of the rubber tree. The white latex oozes out immediately.

23

The history of rubber use

About 250 years ago, when it was discovered that lumps of rubber could rub out pencil marks, people began to investigate what else this interesting substance could be used for.

By 1770 rubber tubing had been made in Europe, and clothes and shoes were being waterproofed with rubber from the Amazon. By 1800 rubber shoes were being sent to the USA, and a factory making ladies' rubber garters was opened in France in 1803.

In 1823 a Scottish chemist called Charles Macintosh discovered a method of making waterproof material using rubber dissolved in a chemical called naptha. Today we still

Their design and rubbery smell made the first macintosh coats rather unpopular. One fashion magazine wrote in 1838: 'No one can look like a gentleman in such a garb and it is of a most unpleasant odour'!

call some waterproof coats 'macs', after Macintosh.

However, there was a problem with this kind of rubber. It became stiff and brittle when cold, and soft and sticky when hot. In 1839 Charles Goodyear discovered that by adding sulphur to rubber and heating the two together (a process called vulcanization), the rubber remained flexible when cold, and no longer melted when hot.

It was shortly after this, in the 1840s, that the first solid rubber tyres were used for horse-drawn carriages, and the transport revolution was born!

I haven't started to cut the bark yet, but I expect dad will teach me in a year or so. At the moment I only help him with the next stage, which is collecting the latex after it has dripped into the cups.

If dad sets out on his longest trail before dawn – at about five o'clock – he doesn't get back home until the sun is almost overhead, at about midday. He's really hungry then, so the first thing he does is to have something to eat. While he's been out in the forest mum will have prepared a meal for him.

What we eat depends mostly on how lucky dad has been at hunting one or two days before. If he has been lucky we might have *paca* stew, or *agouti* with peppers. (*Paca* and *agouti* are small animals, a bit like long-legged guinea pigs.) Sometimes there's a *jacu* (a kind of bird) in delicious sauce, or a piece of venison. If dad brings home a deer,

This is mum in the kitchen, holding Chico. She's boiling some water to make coffee. The hearth we cook on is made of baked clay.

we always share it with Raimundo's family and the other two families that live nearby.

Sometimes there's no meat at all and dad just eats some boiled manioc (like boiled potatoes), or maize, or some *farinha* (which is toasted manioc flour) with gravy, left over from the day before. Occasionally, we have rice that we or another family have grown.

As soon as he has finished his meal and drunk a mug of strong coffee, dad sets off into the forest again. I've started going with him on the shorter trails. This time he takes the metal pail, which the latex that has filled the little cups will be emptied into. He carries a little knapsack on his back, made of blue cotton cloth.

When we get to the rubber trees dad lets me take off the cup, if I can reach it, and pour the latex into the pail. He presses his finger around the inside of the cup so that we get every single drop out. Some of the cups are fixed high up the trees – up to eight metres off the ground. To reach them we have to use a ladder. Our ladders are made out of single poles (often palm tree trunks), with notches cut in them just big enough to hold your toes.

Walking up a ladder with nothing in your hands is not too difficult, but if you are carrying a heavy pail and the pole is wet, it's easy to slip and fall. This happens quite often, and the latex is spilt and wasted.

People get really upset when this happens because the rubber latex takes such a long time to collect.

One thing you have got to look out for when you're in the forest is snakes. Because snakes are cold-blooded they are naturally attracted to anything warm in the forest, especially at night-time, whether it's a large animal or one of us! When dad is cutting the rubber trees very early in the morning before it's light, or collecting the latex after dark, snakes will sometimes come down out of the trees and strike at him as he's climbing the ladder. Rubber tappers carry a little paraffin lamp at night, called a *poronga*. The light and heat of the *poronga* attract the snakes too. I'm afraid of the big snakes, but luckily I haven't been bitten – yet.

One other danger is the jaguars that live in the forest. They could easily kill you if they jumped down on you from the branches of a tree. But generally they keep well away from people, because they are even more frightened of us than we are of them.

We collect three whole pails full of latex from the trees on each trail – that is about eighteen litres of latex in all. Because we've only got one pail, we have to come back to the house when it is full and empty it, then go back into the forest again. By the time we've finished it is late in the afternoon. Dad taps the trees on each trail about once every three days, because each trail takes a day to complete.

Left Here is dad returning home from the forest with a pail full of rubber latex that he has collected.

Cars and the rubber boom

Today, nearly three-quarters of all the natural rubber in the world is used to make rubber tyres. The first tyres were made of solid rubber and so gave carriage passengers a very bumpy ride! But in 1881 John Boyd Dunlop, an Irish vet, successfully used the pneumatic tyre to help his ten-year-old son win a tricycle race. With the development of the motor industry at the end of the last century, there was a sudden demand for more rubber.

The 'Rubber Boom', as it became known, lasted until 1911. Thousands of people travelled to the Amazon to try their hand at tapping the precious latex, but they had no idea what lay in store. Most were very cruelly treated by the bosses whom they were forced to work for. The local Amerindians whose forest was ruthlessly invaded suffered even more. Thousands died from the diseases brought to them by the rubber tappers, and large numbers were enslaved. All this was done so that vehicle tyres could be made.

The businessmen who controlled the rubber trade made enormous fortunes and lived in great luxury. But by 1914 their wealth had disappeared. Rubber from the Amazon was no longer required.

Above The first tyres were made of solid rubber and gave a very bumpy ride! Once pneumatic tyres had been invented (**right**) travelling became more comfortable.

Right This is a black-tufted marmoset — another of the monkeys that live in our reserve. Because these monkeys are so small and agile they are difficult to catch.

Below Dad coming home with an *agouti*. There are lots of these rodents in the forest, so we catch them quite often.

As we walk along the trail we're always on the look out for anything that we can take back home to eat. We walk really quietly so that we don't scare the animals away. Dad can imitate the birds and monkeys just like Uncle Raimundão. They often call back to him and stay nearby. This makes them much easier to catch. Sometimes we don't see any animals at all so we just bring back a piece of honeycomb if we can find it, or some palm fruits if they are easy to knock down.

It's a long and tiring day, but dad's work doesn't end when he gets back home. As soon as we've arrived and he has put his gun and knapsack down, he must begin to turn the latex into a solid rubber block or ball.

So the next thing I'll show you is how he does just that. I hope you don't mind sitting in a cloud of smoke!

29

Making a rubber ball

The first thing that dad does when he gets back from the forest with the latex he has collected is to light a special fire. We have to smoke the latex to turn it into a solid rubber ball. We do this in the smoking hut. It's a little shelter with open sides that Dad built using poles and palm leaf thatch. Nearly all the *seringueiros* have smoking huts like this.

This is the hut where dad turns the latex he has collected into a solid rubber ball.

The rubber tappers here use the old, dry fruit husks of the *cocão* palm to produce the thick white smoke needed to make the latex set. The ones in this picture are fresh and have been cut in half, showing the milky white kernels inside.

On the ground inside the hut is a kind of oven made of clay. It's cone-shaped, with an opening at the side, where you can light the fire, and one at the top to let the smoke out. Because we don't have any paper or matches here, we have to get a light from mum's fire in the kitchen. She keeps that fire going almost all the time if she can – even if the ashes are only just glowing. Sometimes I bring over a piece of smouldering wood which dad will blow on to produce a flame, or we light a little strip of dry rubber in the kitchen and carry it carefully to the hut.

We get the fire going with dry leaves and little sticks. Once it's properly alight we start adding the fuel that will produce really thick white smoke. Everyone round here uses the same thing: old, dry fruits from the *cocão* palm. We collect them when they start

falling from the trees, or pick up old ones when we find them and store them in the hut. They burn slowly and give off the thick white smoke that dad needs to make the latex set.

Dad has a special apparatus set up for smoking the rubber. It's an arrangement of poles and pieces of wood. In front of him, right next to the oven, is a big tin basin, supported on four little wooden poles. Dad tips a pailful of the latex into this, ready for smoking. He puts a long, strong pole in place above the oven, with each end resting on wooden supports. This pole will hold the rubber ball that he's about to make. Then he threads a round section of banana tree trunk on to the pole and pushes it to the middle. This piece of trunk will start off the round shape of the ball.

Before he begins, dad makes sure that a good thick plume of smoke is billowing out of the oven. Then, sitting on a bar at the side of the oven, he picks up one end of the pole with the banana wood on. With his left hand he begins to turn the pole round and round, holding it over the basin, and making sure that it does not slip off the support at the other end. With his right hand he scoops up a gourd full of the latex in the basin, and quickly tips it over the banana wood. He moves the pole immediately so that the banana wood, which is now coated with white latex, is directly in the line of the smoke, and keeps it turning.

As if by magic, the liquid latex starts to go thick and set. It forms a yellowish-white coat around the banana wood cylinder. Dad has to keep on scooping gourds full of the latex from the basin and tipping them over the

Right Here you can see the basin full of latex, next to the oven, and the gourd that dad uses to scoop the latex out and over the ball he is making.

Left This shows dad tipping more latex over the ball. He keeps the ball turning as he does this, to make sure that it is evenly coated.

cylinder like this, making sure that any latex that drips off falls back into the basin. And he must keep turning the pole, to make sure that an even rubber coating is formed. It's really hard work!

Once the rubber coating has built up to about one inch thick, dad stops. He quickly takes the pole off the support and out of the smoke and pushes the banana wood cylinder off. Then he takes his knife and cuts the soft rubber – which feels slippery and wet – off the banana wood in three strips. He wraps these strips directly around the middle of the pole, where the cylinder was before. In this way he makes a rounded, cylinder shape of rubber which will form the centre of a great big rubber ball.

After pouring each gourdful of latex over the ball, dad quickly moves the pole supporting it over the oven. The smoke makes the rubber congeal.

Then dad puts the pole back in position and begins all over again, tipping the latex over the ball and holding it in the smoke until all the liquid has been used up. By the time he has finished, the ball is pretty big and very heavy. The effect of the smoke has turned the rubber dark brown in colour – almost black.

Each day, when he returns from the forest, dad tips more latex over the ball until it has reached the right size. It takes about 100 litres of latex to make a ball that big.

Smoking rubber is very hot and tiring work, but the worst thing you have to put up with is the smoke. If there is even a slight breeze the smoke goes everywhere. It is impossible not to breathe it in, and sometimes we can't stop coughing. It's like being trapped in a room with a bonfire!

There is another way to make the latex solid though, without using smoke at all, which is to use *ofé* sap. The *ofé* is a huge tree that grows in the forest. One of the *seringueiros* discovered that if you mixed a little of the sap of this tree with the rubber latex it has a similar effect to when latex is smoked, making it thick and solid. So the rubber tappers use either this method or the smoking one like dad, and some use both.

Branches of an *ofé* tree. The trees can grow up to 40 metres tall. *Ofé* sap is used to thicken latex and make it solid.

In general, people prefer to use *ofé* because it means that they don't have to breathe smoke in all the time. Some people use *ofé* because it's hard for them to find the *cocão* fruits for fuel and it saves using wood from the forest instead.

After mixing a little tin cupful of *ofé* sap with each pailful of latex you simply wait for it to thicken. Then when it has begun to set, you tip it into a wooden box and place a lid on top. As you press the lid down, it squeezes the water out and leaves a solid rubber block.

All the rubber tappers in this part of the reserve have to carry the blocks or balls of rubber on their backs to the new community warehouse at Foz do Jacaré. It's extremely hard work because the blocks weigh about 40 kilos each. But at least dad can exchange our rubber fairly for some of the things we need, now that the co-operative has been set up.

Here is dad with a block of rubber he has made by mixing latex with ofé sap and then pressing it in the wooden box.

Before we had the co-operative – only a short time ago – life here was much worse for everybody. The *patrão*, Da Silva, made dad and all the others work for nothing. He demanded that each *seringueiro* pay 70 kilos of rubber to him for each trail they tapped, just as a sort of rent.

On top of that, instead of paying us for the rest of the rubber we produced, Da Silva cheated us. He would offer to sell us a bag of salt or rice, or some cartridges for dad's gun, but we had to pay four or five times more than these things really cost. Because we

Rubber plantations

The rubber tree (*Hevea brasiliensis*) is native to the Amazon rainforest. But in the nineteenth century, the British decided they wanted to grow rubber trees for themselves. Getting seeds from Brazil, in 1876 the British set up plantations in Malaysia. By 1914 Malaysian rubber had become so cheap that no one in Europe or the USA wanted to buy rubber harvested from wild trees in the Amazon. Lots of rubber tappers left the forest and returned to their original homes.

During the Second World War – when Britain and the USA could not get rubber from Malaysia – there was a small revival of the industry in Brazil. People moved to the forest again to tap the trees. Although this boom did not last long, many men and women stayed.

Nearly three-quarters of the world's natural rubber is used to make tyres. For many products natural rubber is still preferred to synthetic rubber.

There are at least 100,000 rubber tappers in the Amazon region of Brazil today. Almost all the latex they collect is used in South America. Brazil now grows rubber in plantations too, outside the rainforest. Many rubber tappers are worried that in the future their rubber won't be needed, because rubber from plantations will be cheaper. Plantation trees are grown close together in straight lines and so they are easier to tap. Chemicals are sometimes used to make more latex flow from the trees.

Not all the rubber that is used for industry today comes from trees. Synthetic rubber is made out of chemicals from coal and oil. But, although synthetic rubber has many important uses (such as the treads for car tyres), natural rubber is superior in certain ways. Natural rubber is stronger and doesn't get so hot when it is continually bent or flexed. It keeps its shape well while it is being moulded. The world uses around 5 million tonnes of natural rubber each year – for everything from surgeon's gloves to high-speed train tyres in Japan!

A rubber tree plantation.

Dad with a small amount of rubber that has just been smoked. This is only about half the size of the rubber ball that he usually carries to the community warehouse.

don't have any money at all, he would say that we could pay him later with rubber. Every few months Da Silva would present my dad with a bill: an amount of rubber that he said dad owed. Although dad has never learned to read or write, he knew that the amount was wrong. It was always more than we could ever collect. So we were always in debt to him, and never got paid.

Once, when dad said he couldn't possibly collect all the rubber Da Silva was asking for, a man appeared at our house with a gun. He threatened us and pushed my dad and broke our radio, the only special thing we had.

Now, at last, the forest is ours and things have changed. Dad says there are exciting things in store for us!

A new life in the forest

Thanks to the efforts of the rubber tappers this region has been made into a reserve, and we can't be pushed out of the forest by anyone. There are still lots of powerful cattle ranchers and timber merchants who would like to take our land, but the Brazilian president himself decreed that the forest was ours to use, and this has helped stop them. Some of our relatives from other parts of the forest haven't been so lucky, and now they are living in shacks down by the river in Cruzeiro do Sul.

This is what our forest would have looked like if Da Silva had had his way: hardly any trees, and unhappy cattle looking for grass.

This trader has become wealthy by selling rubber. Most of the rubber blocks around him are made up of smaller pieces that have been pressed together.

The best thing for us is that Da Silva has left. Instead of having to depend on him and the traders for most of our supplies, which got every family round here into debt, we now have the co-operative. The co-operative is a kind of community business, that all the families in the area have a share in. We are all involved in how it is run, and we share everything that happens as a result. I'll explain how it works.

All the *seringueiros* carry their rubber to the base at Foz do Jacaré. Here, it is weighed and the amount brought in by each person is recorded in a book. The rubber is then taken in one of the co-operative boats to Cruzeiro do Sul, where it will be sold. We get a much better price for it like this than Da Silva ever told us he could get. The co-operative's representative uses the money earned from selling the rubber to buy the goods that the community needs. These things are brought back to Foz do Jacaré by boat. Having the co-operative means that each family can now get things much more cheaply, to match the value of the rubber they have collected. So you see, it's an exchange system, which works well.

Of course, until recently the rubber tappers here didn't have boats of their own or co-operative buildings. We have these things now because the *seringueiros* made a careful plan. They wrote all their ideas down and decided to ask the government if it would help. The plan was called 'Community Development for the Armadillo River'.

Right This rubber tree and all the others in our reserve have formed our way of life. We respect the forest and all its different trees because they will shape our future too.

Above When this building – at Foz do Jacaré – is finished, it will be our new community office and store.

Right This is dad making a broom from *açu* and *titica* vines.

In the plan they described how difficult things have been here for everyone; how the rubber bosses forced us to live like slaves without allowing us any schools or health care. They asked for enough money to set up the co-operative. They wanted to construct warehouses to store the rubber, as well as buildings for meetings at different places along the Armadillo river, and a headquarters building in Cruzeiro do Sul. They also wanted boats for carrying people, goods and rubber.

The plan explained that we would like schools and health posts here in the reserve. It also described how we would like to be able to process and sell some of the other things that the forest provides plenty of, like different palm fruits and honey, as well as natural rubber.

The Brazilian Government gave us enough money to start to do these things, which is how we got some of the buildings and the boats. But it was not enough for everything. Dad says that because lots of people have heard what we are trying to do, living in the forest and protecting it, we will probably get a bit more money. I hope that it will be enough to build the school and health posts that we need, and to start some projects using things the forest provides.

The importance of wild rubber trees

Although most of the world's rubber now comes from trees raised in plantations in Asia, the wild trees that grow in the Amazon are extremely important to the rubber industry.

Because wild rubber trees have been scattered over such a large area for such a long time, individual trees have developed in special ways. Some produce more latex than others, and some are more resistant to disease. Scientists have been collecting the seeds of these trees to cross them with those grown commercially, to help plantation trees to do better.

So the rubber tappers in the Amazon are doing a very important job – protecting the wild trees and the forest in which they grow. Sadly, very large areas containing rubber trees of many different kinds have been cut down and burnt over the last ten years. Ranchers and timber companies have done most of the damage, along with the poor colonists encouraged to move to the rainforest in search of land.

I don't know what a school is like. Neither do my mum or dad. Nobody from Mato Grosso has ever been to one. Dad says that schools are very important because they teach you lots of useful things, like how to read and write. We don't have any books or paper here at home, or any pencils or pens, but I've seen them at Foz do Jacaré. Mum is worried about us going to school. She wants to know who will help her with her work, and who will help my dad. The first school will be built at Foz do Jacaré, I think. Then there will be others throughout our reserve. I'm looking forward to learning how to read and write and to draw pictures.

Bringing supplies from town to the reserve. The co-operative now has several boats for carrying people, rubber and supplies.

Mum says she thinks the best thing will be having medicines to treat us when we get ill or hurt ourselves. At the moment there are no medicines here at all. When Maria Nazaré was just about to be born, mum got very ill and there was nothing anyone could do. Dad was frightened that she would die. The nearest hospital is in Cruzeiro do Sul, and it takes four days by boat to get there. We had no money to pay for her to go, and even if we had there were no boats available. It was a miracle, dad said, that she survived and that Maria Nazaré was born alive and well.

When we get a health post in the reserve, we will be able to go for help if we get ill, or get diseases like malaria. There will be medicines for snake bites and for sting ray wounds. I can't wait for that!

In order to be able to keep on buying medicines for the health post and other things the community needs, we want to see if we can make things that people outside the forest would like to buy. We could gather honey from the forest bees, putting up hives for them in the trees; we could collect fruits from the *patoá* and *coco açu* and lots of other palms, and press out the oil or juice from them, or make different sorts of flour; we could make brooms or baskets or furniture from vines; and make delicious sweets from the fruits of forest trees. And then, of course, there are brazil nuts!

Rubber tappers and Amerindians gather nearly all the brazil nuts that are eaten around the world. Selling them gives many people an important income.

These little shoes were made here in this forest. They are soft and comfortable to wear. We hope to make more shoes like these. One day, perhaps, I'll make a pair for you!

There are so many things that we could do if we had equipment to help us and some sturdy animals to help carry the heavy loads. As well as producing the rubber balls and blocks, we'd like to make things out of rubber, the rubber that we tap from the trees right here. We could make rubber boots, or soft rubber shoes. Or we could make toys for boys and girls who live in other countries of the world. I'm looking forward to my life here in the forest, with all the trees and animals and birds, and with all our friends and relatives around us.

So next time you see something made of natural rubber – like the tyres of all the vehicles and aeroplanes in the world, which my dad has told me about – think of us here in the forest, protecting the rubber trees!

Defending the forest

Antonio and his family and friends are luckier than most rubber tapper families. Because the area of forest they live in has been made into an extractive reserve they will be able to protect it for many years to come. But the reserve was only officially decreed because the *seringueiros* fought for the right to protect it and to stop the people who were exploiting them and threatening to cut the forest down.

Many rubber tappers have died trying to save their forest, and the battle still continues today.

Looking forward to the future: me with my sisters, Maria Nazaré and Maria Aparecida.

Glossary

Armadillo   An animal with strong claws for digging, whose body is covered in horny plates. Armadillos can roll themselves into a ball for protection.

Co-operative   A business owned and run by a group of people with profits shared between them.

Extractive reserve   An area of forest in which local people can live and work, harvesting natural forest products like rubber and brazil nuts.

Estrada (say es-trar-da)   Rubber tappers' trails in the forest.

Farinha (say fa-reen-ya)   A coarse flour made by grating and then toasting manioc roots. *Farinha* is eaten at most meal times by rubber tappers.

Gourd   The hollow, hard skin of the fruit of the calabash tree. It is commonly used in the Amazon forest as a bowl, or water container.

Hardwoods   Broad-leaved trees, which shed their leaves during the year.

Jacuruxi (say ja-coo-roo-shee)   A lizard native to the Amazon rainforest.

Latex   The white sap of the rubber tree which the rubber tappers collect and turn into rubber balls and blocks.

Machete   A heavy knife with a long, broad blade, often used in South America as a tool for clearing undergrowth.

Maize   The cereal plant, also called corn, which produces large grains set in rows on a cob.

Manioc   The main root crop eaten by people in the Amazon rainforest. There are many different kinds of manioc. (It is also called cassava.)

Patrão (say pa-trow)   The owner or boss in charge of an area of rubber trees (a rubber estate).

Patrões (say pa-troy-ish)   The plural of *patrão*. The *patrões* are still very powerful in many parts of the forest where there are no extractive reserves.

Plantation   An estate where trees are farmed.

Pneumatic tyre   A rubber tyre filled with air under pressure.

Sap   The juice or fluid found in living plants and trees.

Seringa (say se-reen-ga)   The Portuguese word for rubber latex, the sap of the rubber tree.

Seringuiera (say se-reen-ge-ra)   A rubber tree. The botanical name is *Hevea brasiliensis*.

Seringuiero (say se-reen-ge-ro)   A rubber tapper. Although most rubber tappers are men, some women work as rubber tappers too.

Synthetic   Something that is artificially made, not natural.

Tinamou   A brown or grey South American bird similar to a grouse, which spends most of its time on the forest floor.

Tucandera ant (say too-can-de-ra)   A large ant found in the rainforest. Its name comes from its long biting jaws which remind local people of a toucan's bill.

Uru bird (say oo-roo)   The wood quail, native to South and Central America. It has a short tail and its bill is strong and serrated (notched like a saw).

Vulcanization   The process of heating natural rubber together with sulphur. This makes the rubber harder and stronger.

Further information

Conserving Rainforests by Martin Banks
(Wayland, 1989)
*Fight for the forest: Chico Mendes in his own
words* (Latin American Bureau, 1989)
Jungles and Rainforests by Theodore
Rowland-Entwistle (Wayland, 1987)
Rainforest Amerindians by Anna Lewington
(Wayland, 1992)

*White Gold: The diary of a rubber cutter in the
Amazon 1906-16* by J. C. Yungjohann
(Synergetic Press, 1989)
Available from WWF (see address below):
audio cassette, word booklet and score of the
musical *Yanomamo* (about the Amazon basin
and the rainforest), also a video of the musical,
entitled *Song of the Forest.*

The following organizations can send you more information about tropical rainforests, and the
people that live in them:

Friends of the Earth
26–28 Underwood Street
London
N1 7JQ

Living Earth Foundation
The Old Laundry
Ossington Buildings
Moxon Street
London
W1M 3JD

OXFAM
274 Banbury Road
Oxford
OX2 7DZ

Rainforest Foundation
2 Ingate Place
Battersea
London
SW8 3NS

Survival International
310 Edgeware Road
London
W2 1DY

World Wide Fund for Nature (WWF)
Panda House
Weyside Park
Catteshall Lane
Godalming
Surrey
GU7 1XR

All pictures supplied by Edward Parker, except Mary Evans Picture Library (8), Marion and Tony Morrison (12), Wayland
Picture Library (28). Artwork supplied by Peter Bull (5, 9, 19), Jackie Harland (14, 21, 32), John Yates (24).

Index